At the Beach

Eric Bradley

You can find all kinds of
things at the beach.

You can sort the things you find.

Put all the shells together.

Put all the rocks together.

Put all the seaweed together.

Put all the driftwood together.

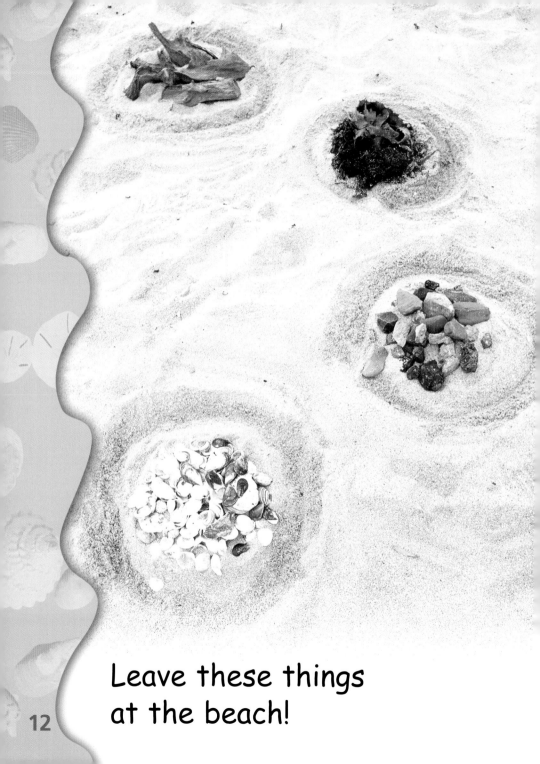

Leave these things
at the beach!